W9-CFQ-208

1·2·3
I Can Collage!

Irene Luxbacher

KIDS CAN PRESS

A collage is ART you make by gluing paper, photographs and other colorful things onto another piece of paper. It can look like something real or something you imagine.
Let's collage sea creatures …

The things you use to make a collage are called
MATERIALS.

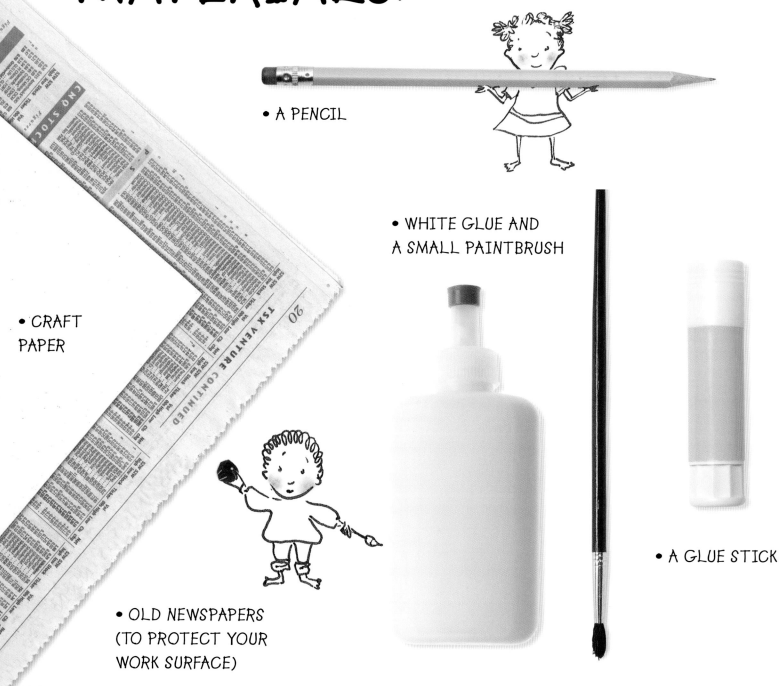

• A PENCIL

• WHITE GLUE AND
A SMALL PAINTBRUSH

• CRAFT
PAPER

• A GLUE STICK

• OLD NEWSPAPERS
(TO PROTECT YOUR
WORK SURFACE)

4

• SCRAPS OF PAPER: WRAPPING PAPER, WALL PAPER, SANDPAPER, CONSTRUCTION PAPER, OLD NEWSPAPERS AND MAGAZINES, OLD DRAWINGS AND PAINTINGS, TISSUE PAPER, ETC.

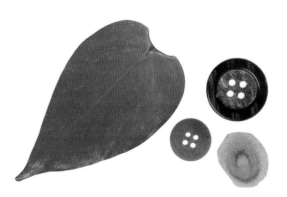

• FOUND OBJECTS

• MARKERS

• SCISSORS

ARTIST'S SECRET:

Start a collection of all different kinds of paper or paper scraps. Keep them all in one place so they're handy when you're ready to start your collage!

5

CUT It OUT

Snip, snip, snip! Cut some SIMPLE SHAPES out of scrap paper to make this colorful collage of a flying fish!

1. Use scissors to cut out lots of small circles for your fish's colorful scales. Next cut out two triangles for your fish's head and tail. Then cut out two smaller triangles for your fish's fins.

2. On a big piece of craft paper, use a pencil to draw a large banana shape for the outline of your fish's body.

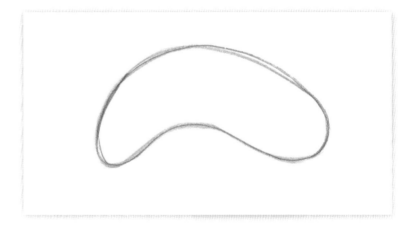

3. Glue on the bigger triangles for the head and tail. Glue on the other two triangles for the fins. Glue the circles in rows so that they touch and overlap like a fish's scales.

SPLOOSH!
A Flying Fish!

Cut and glue two very small circles for your flying fish's eyes.
Use a marker to draw your fish's eyeball and a smiling mouth.
Glue some scraps of blue tissue paper along the bottom of the
paper for big ocean waves that your fish can leap in and out of.

A collage made using pieces of
paper cut into different shapes is
called a CUT PAPER COLLAGE.

7

TEAR It UP

Tear into this idea! All it takes is some RIPPED UP paper to make a collage of an eight-armed octopus!

1. Tear a large circle out of colored paper for your octopus's head and body. (Don't worry if it's not perfectly round.) Glue it onto a large piece of craft paper.

2. Tear eight long, thin paper strips out of tissue or construction paper for your octopus's arms. Glue them around your octopus's body. (If you like, you can tuck the edges of the arms under your octopus's head and body.)

3. Tear a few small circles out of scraps of paper and glue them onto your octopus's body to add a few silly spots.

OH! An Awesome Octopus!

Add a friendly face to your octopus by gluing on more ripped paper to make eyes, cheeks, a smiling mouth and teeth. For a finishing touch, use a marker to draw lots of little circles along your octopus's arms for its suction cups.

A collage made out of paper that has been torn or ripped into different shapes is called a TORN PAPER COLLAGE.

PICTURE It

Did you know that you can turn a whole bunch of pictures into one big one? Use cutouts from old PHOTOS and MAGAZINES to make this whale of a collage!

1. Use a pencil or marker to draw a big oval on a large piece of craft paper. Cut out your whale's body.

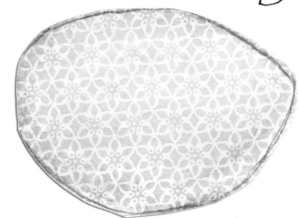

2. Carefully cut out some interesting and colorful pictures from old photos and magazines that you've collected. Using a plastic container and a paintbrush, stir a big spoonful of white glue into 125 mL (½ c.) of water.

3. Brush a bit of the glue mixture onto a small area of your whale, and press on a few cutouts. Brush a bit more of the mixture over the cutouts, making sure the edges are nice and flat. Cover your whole whale with cutouts this way.

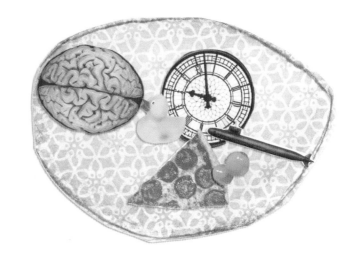

WHOA! A Whopper of a Whale!

With a paintbrush or your fingers, paint a wavy ocean on another piece of craft paper. Once it's dry, glue on your collaged whale. Give it a cutout tail, and use markers to draw on a mouth and a blowhole. What a happy humpback!

Brushing a mixture of white glue and water over a cut or torn paper collage is called DECOUPAGE.

LOST and FOUND

Look around — inside and outside your home. What CREATIVE COLLAGE MATERIALS will you find? Look for fallen leaves, buttons, scraps of fabric, beads and string to make this crabby collage!

1. Cut a large circle out of a piece of colored construction paper. This is your crab's shell. Glue it onto a large piece of craft paper.

2. Arrange a few different kinds of leaves or grass around your shell for your crab's head, legs and front pincers. Glue them in place.

3. Glue on your collection of fabric, beads and string to give your crab a shell full of fun spots.

HEY! A Cute Crab!

Look for a couple beads or buttons to glue on for your crab's eyes. Then find small sticks or twigs to glue on for its antennae. Glue long strips cut out of sandpaper or a brown paper bag along the bottom of the paper to make a super sandy shore for your crab to run along.

FOUND OBJECTS are art materials you find just by looking around you. They are things you think are special, even if other people might not.

13

Pretty PATTERNS

Look through your collection of SCRAP PAPER to find some neat patterns for a collage of a starfish family. (Hint: Pieces of used wrapping paper often have FUN PATTERNS.)

1. Use a pencil to draw four or five stars on a sand-colored piece of paper. Try making them a few different sizes and not too small. And don't worry if they don't all look exactly the same — it's better that way!

2. Carefully cut out each star. Ask an adult helper to poke through the paper with your scissors to get you started. (You can save the cutout stars for another day.)

3. Spread out your collection of patterned paper. Lay the sand-colored paper on top so the patterned paper shows through the cutout stars. Move the patterned paper around until you like the way your starfish family looks. One at a time, glue the patterned paper in place.

SILLY!
A Starfish Family!

Use cutouts and a marker to add faces on your starfish family. Tear a long strip of blue paper and glue it along the top of the sand-colored paper to add watery waves.

A **PATTERN** is repeated decoration or design. The design on a piece of wrapping paper is a pattern.

UNDER, Over, Under, OVER

Weave a collage that looks like the shell of a shy little sea turtle!

1. Cut a large oval out of green or brown construction paper for your sea turtle's shell. Starting at one edge, make four or five cuts across the oval, stopping just before you cut through the other edge. Then cut some strips of colored paper.

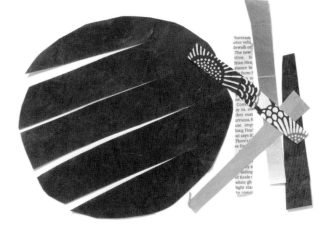

2. Slide a strip of paper down through the first cut in the shell. Then pull it up through the second cut. Keep weaving the strip under and over like this until you reach the edge of the shell. Do this with each strip until the shell is finished. Trim the ends that peek over the shell's edges.

3. Cut five small ovals out of the leftover brown or green construction paper. Glue on two ovals for your turtle's front legs, two ovals for its back legs and the last oval for its head.

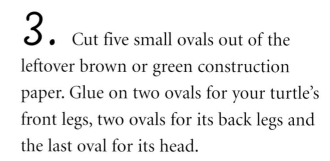

PEEK-A-BOO!
A Shy Sea Turtle!

Cut and glue on a small triangle of construction paper for your turtle's little tail. Glue your turtle onto another piece of paper. Finally, cut and glue on a pair of eyes so your sea turtle can see you, too!

When you slide a strip of paper under and over other strips of paper you are WEAVING.

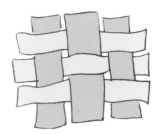

17

AMAZING Ocean Animal

Imagine the **SUPER SEA CREATURE** you could make if you put all your collage techniques together into one amazing idea! How about a water-breathing sea dragon?

BODY (PART 1)

Cut out a big, squiggly body from a piece of brightly colored paper. Try to make sure there's a wide end (the body) and a narrow end (the tail).

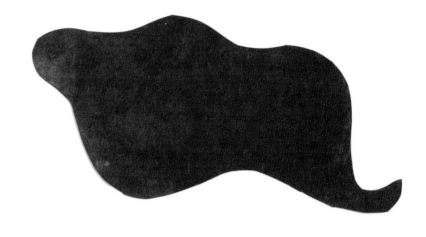

BODY (PART 2)

Make a few cuts across the widest part of the body, starting at one edge but stopping just before you cut through the other edge. Cut out a few strips of colorful paper and weave them in and out of your sea dragon's body.

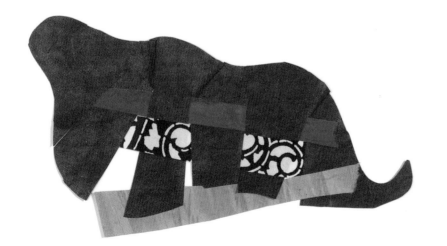

HEAD AND SNOUT

What objects can you find to glue on for the head and snout? What about a round or oval leaf for the head and a piece of grass, a stick or a twig for its snout?

WINGS

Tear two wings out of another piece of brightly colored paper. Glue them to your sea dragon's body.

OCEAN

Collect some pieces of colorful paper that remind you of the ocean and the ocean floor. Glue them onto a big piece of craft paper for an ocean background. Next, glue on your dragon. Cut some fun pictures out of old photos and magazines, and glue them around your sea dragon.

CORAL

Cut some ovals or small stars out of the ocean background. (Ask an adult helper to carefully poke through the paper with scissors to get you started.) Place the background over scraps of patterned wrapping paper for some crazy-looking coral. One at a time, glue the patterned papers in place.

19

A DAZZLING Sea Dragon!

Give your sea dragon eyes by gluing on two beads or buttons. Cut out small paper circles and glue colorful spots and scales on your sea dragon's wings and body. Glue on some long grass stems for seaweed and pieces of sandpaper for a sandy ocean bottom.

MIXED MEDIA COLLAGE is a collage made using different kinds of materials, such as cut and torn paper, as well as found objects.

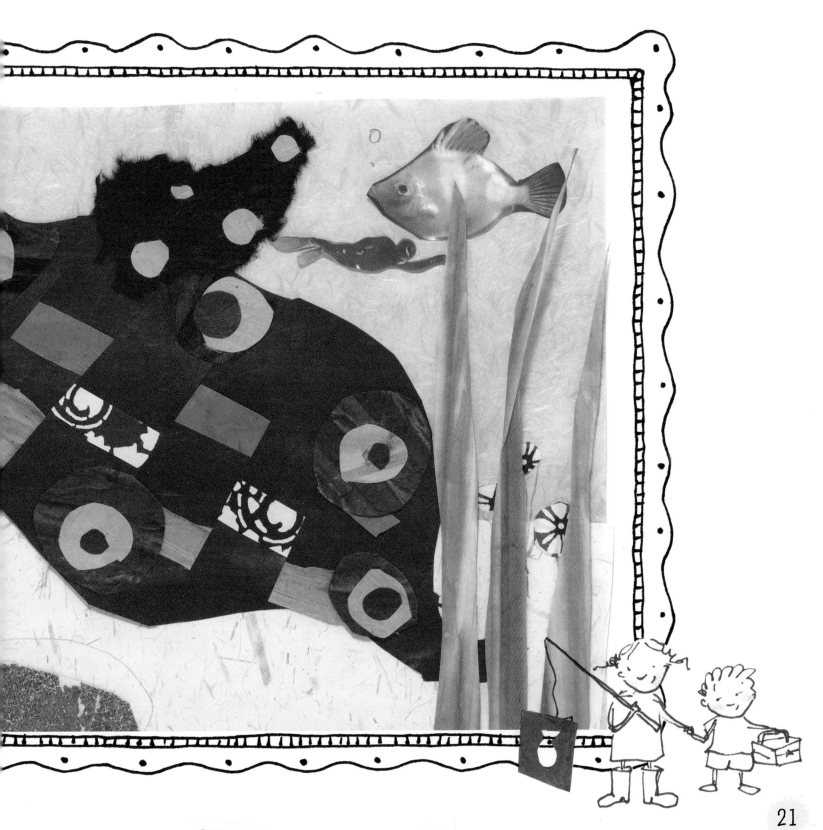

Note to PARENTS and TEACHERS

We chose sea creatures as a fun theme for exploring some basic collage techniques, but there are lots of other topics or themes you can use to inspire your young artist. Here are a few ideas to get you started.

• Make a collage of your favorite flowers. Tear some long tissue paper stems and glue them to a blue paper sky background (see Tear It Up, page 8). For petals, cut out a few colorful circles and ovals from old magazines or wrapping paper and glue them to the top of each stem (see Cut It Out, page 6). Glue buttons, beads or pom-poms in the center of your flowers (see Lost and Found, page 12). Add some insects, fairies or tiny people cut out of magazines to finish off your garden of fun flowers (see Picture It, page 10)!

• Or you can collage a self-portrait. Cut a large oval out of a piece of construction paper. Keep the piece with the oval cutout and put the oval aside for another day. Choose another piece of paper for your face and glue it to the back of the paper (see Pretty Patterns, page 14). Tear and glue torn tissue paper for your hair (see Tear It Up, page 8). Cut out and glue on simple shapes from colorful paper scraps: circles for your eyes, ovals for your ears, a triangle for your nose and a half circle for your mouth (see Cut It Out, page 6). Gather buttons, beads and fabric pieces (see Lost and Found, page 12) or magazine cutouts (see Picture It, page 10) to add hair ribbons, jewelry, teeth, eyebrows, eyelashes and a hat or scarf to your funny face!

Tips to ensure a GOOD COLLAGE EXPERIENCE every time:

1. Use inexpensive materials and make sure your young artist's clothes and the work area are protected from spills. This way it's all about the fun, not the waste and the mess.

2. Focus on the process rather than the end product. Make sure your young artist is relaxed and having fun with the information instead of expecting perfection every time.

3. Remind your young artist that mistakes are an artist's best friend. The most interesting collage ideas and paper combinations are often discovered by mistake.

COLLAGE Words

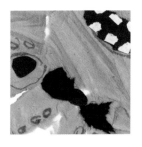

23

FOR NOAH AND ELIJAH

Special thanks to Stacey Roderick and Karen Powers. This book would not have been possible without their amazing talents and insights.

Kids Can Press acknowledges the financial support of the Government of Ontario, through the Ontario Media Development Corporation's Ontario Book Initiative, and the Government of Canada, through the BPIDP, for our publishing activity.

Published in Canada by
Kids Can Press Ltd.
29 Birch Avenue
Toronto, ON M4V 1E2

Published in the U.S. by
Kids Can Press Ltd.
2250 Military Road
Tonawanda, NY 14150

www.kidscanpress.com

Kids Can Press is a Corus™ Entertainment company

Edited by Stacey Roderick
Designed by Karen Powers

Photos on pages 4–5: Ray Boudreau
(except scissors: © iStockphoto.com/Mark Yuill)
Printed and bound in Singapore

The paper used to print this book was produced with elemental chlorine-free pulp, harvested from managed sustainable forests.

The hardcover edition of this book is smyth sewn casebound. The paperback edition of this book is limp sewn with a drawn-on cover.

CM 09 0 9 8 7 6 5 4 3 2 1
CM PA 09 0 9 8 7 6 5 4 3 2 1

Library and Archives Canada Cataloguing in Publication

Luxbacher, Irene, 1970–
        123 I can collage! / written and illustrated by
Irene Luxbacher.

(Starting art)
ISBN 978-1-55453-313-8 (bound).
ISBN 978-1-55453-314-5 (pbk.)

1. Collage—Technique—Juvenile literature. I. Title. II. Title: One, two, three I can collage! III. Series: Luxbacher, Irene, 1970– Starting art.

N7433.7.L89 2009   j702.81'2   C2008-903250-0